C000245498

BE HAPPY

By the same author:

Do you love me?
Late have I loved you
One of those who said Yes
With all my love
The golden rule

MARIAROSA GUERRINI O.S.A.

THE BEATITUDES

ST PAULS

Original title: *Beatitudini ...dei saggi*
© Editrice Rogate, Roma

Translated by Thomas Kala

Cover by Mary Lou Winters fsp

ST PAULS Publishing
187 Battersea Bridge Road, London SW11 3AS, UK
www.stpauls.ie

English translation © ST PAULS 1992

ISBN 085439 409 5

First published 1992. Reprinted 1994, 2001

Printed by The Guernsey Press Co. Ltd, Guernsey, C.I.

ST PAULS is an activity of the priests and brothers of
the Society of St Paul who proclaim the Gospel through the media
of social communication

For those
who seek
the secret of
happiness

The God of love
has placed
the key to happiness
in our own hearts.

If the springs of happiness
are within our hearts,
why do we find it difficult
to fill our lives with joy?

St Augustine shares
this secret with us:

> People go to great lengths
> to admire
> the majesty
> of mountains
> and the power
> of the waves of the sea,
> the beauty of waterfalls,
> the vastness of the oceans,
> the revolution of the planets,
> but they never pause
> to wonder at the mystery
> of their own hearts.
>   (Confessions, 10:8,15)

They are like those
who set out to explore
the city centre,
and then,
forgetting it,
wander on the outskirts.

And yet,
none can deny
the longing,
in the heart of their hearts,
to be happy!

How can you find happiness?
With unhurried pace,
turn the pages of this little book.
Between a reflection,
a smile,
a thought,
and a simple prayer...
you may perhaps find
the path to happiness.

Join us and climb the mountain,
where,
Jesus our brother,
JOY OF NATIONS,
told us,
we will find
true joy,
the joy of the heart.
The path is steep,
the conditions are hard,
the price is high.

We must be FREE
to enjoy it.
We must become WORTHY
to find it,
and above all
we must be BRAVE
to seize it.

The Augustinian Sisters

Happy
are those...

Happy are the poor

... for theirs is
the Kingdom of
Heaven.

Happy are those who mourn

... for they shall be
comforted.

Happy are the meek

... for they will inherit
the earth.

Happy are those who hunger and thirst for what is right

... for they shall
be satisfied.

Happy are the merciful

... for they will obtain
mercy.

Happy are the pure in heart

... for they shall
see God.

Happy are the peacemakers

... for they will be called
the children of God.

Happy are the persecuted

... for their reward
will be great
in heaven.

Jesus spoke of happiness
   not only on the mountain...

But on every path,
at the crossroads
and squares,
at every corner,
indoors and outdoors.

Jesus promised happiness...
on certain conditions!

Happy are those who believe without seeing!

John 20:29

Happy are those servants whose master finds them awake on his return.

I assure you, he will take of his coat, make them sit at his table, and will wait on them.

Luke 12:37

Happy are those who have no doubts about me.

JESUS

Matthew 11:6

Happy are those
who suffer
in patience.

You have hear of
Job's patience,
and you know
how the Lord
rewarded him
in the end.

For the Lord
is full of
mercy
and compassion.

James 5:11

Happy are you
when you
suffer insults
for following
Christ,

for it is a sign
that the
Spirit of God
rests upon you.

1 Peter 4:14

Happy are you
when you suffer
for doing
what is right.

Do not be afraid
of anyone,
and do not worry,
but praise the Lord
in your hearts.

At all times
be ready
to show
why you hope
in the Lord.

1 Peter 3:14

41

Perhaps so far
you've been thinking
that only a few,
the 'herdes',
ever find happiness –
but here's
another little tip:

The Lord of laughter and joy
asks us to use
a little 'good sense'
in our daily life.

Buried in the heap
of mounting little occasions
of GOOD SENSE
there is a treasure chest
of happiness.

All we need to do
is a pinch
of the spice of faith
to whatever we do.

Happy are you
if you can
laugh at yourself.

All your problems
will then vanish
like a mirage.

Happy
are you
when you get
neither blame
nor praise.

Then paths will
light up for you
even as you look.

Happy are you
if you can
think well
of others
even in the face
of evidence
to the contrary.

You may be
taken for a fool,
but that's the price
you must pay
for charity.

Happy are you
    when you recognize
    the Lord
    in all those
    you meet,

    for then you have
    true wisdom
    and understanding.

Happy are you

if you can keep
your peace
and smile
when all around you
shout and scream
and tread
on your corns,

for it is a sign
that your heart
is opening
to the Gospel.

Happy are you

if you can pay
due attention
to little things
and deal calmly
with big things,

for you will make
great progress
in life.

Happy

are you
if you can
treasure a smile
and ignore
an insult,

for then
the sun
will shine
on your path.

Happy are those
who think
and pray
before acting,

for they
will avoid
many blunders.

Happy are those
who come
to the aid
of others
and still know
they are not
indispensable,

for they will
bring
true happiness
to others.

Happy are those who are wise enough not to take themselves too seriously,

for everyone will be at ease in their company.

Happy are those
who know
how to be quiet
and listen,

for they
will then grow
in knowledge.

Happy are those
who can relax
and sleep
without
worrying,

for they
will become
wise.

Happy are those
who know
that a molehill
is not
a mountain,

for they
will be spared
much bother
and embarrassment.

Happy are those
who can see
the funny side
of things,

for they
will never
be bored.

Humanity has always
sought happiness.
The scriptures,
especially the Psalms,
assure us
that we can
find happiness;
but we must believe
and pursue it.

Many people
are desperate
to find
happiness;
but they must
stop waiting around
and set out
in search of
happiness.

Happy are those who protect the weak,

in the hour
of need
the Lord
will come
to their aid.

Psalm 40:2

Happy are those
who find
strength
in you,
O Lord,
and adhere
to your path.

As they pass
through
the dry valley
it becomes
a place of springs.

Psalm 84:6

Happy are those
who dwell
in your house,
O Lord.

For ever
they sing
your praise.

Psalm 84:5

Happy are those
who put
their trust
in the Lord
and shun
the company
of the proud-hearted
and the deceitful.

Psalm 40:5

Happy are those
who acclaim you,
O Lord,
and walk
in the light
of your countenance.

All day long
they rejoice
in your name.

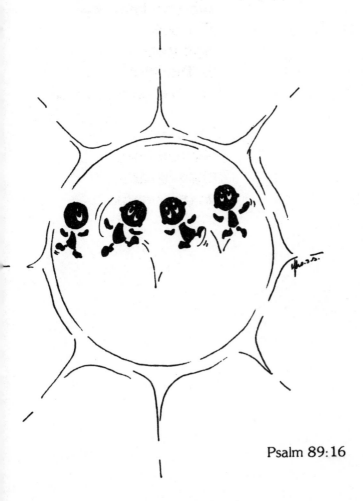

Psalm 89:16

Happy are those
who are generous
with their loans,
who are honest
in their dealings.

They will always
be steadfast
and will be
remembered
for ever.

Psalm 112:5

Happy are those
who honour
the Lord,
who find delight
in obeying
his commandments.

Their children
will be powerful
on earth,
and their descendants
will be blessed.

Psalm 112:1

Happy are those who act justly and always do what is right.

Psalm 106:3

Happy are those
whom the Lord
instructs
in his laws,

so that they
may find
refuge
in times of trouble.

Psalm 94:12

Happy are those
who do
no evil
in the sight
of the Lord
and who are
free
from all deceit.

Psalm 32:2

Happy are those
whose faults
are pardoned,
whose sins
are forgiven.

Psalm 32:1

Happy are those
who reject
the counsel
of the wicked,
who do not follow
the example
of sinners
or seek
the company
of scoffers.

They are like trees
on river banks
who bear fruit
in season,
and their leaves
never dry up.

Psalm 1:1

Happy are those
whom the Lord
has blessed
with children
for children
are like arrows
in the hand
of a warrior.

Happy are those
who have
many such arrows,
they will never be
defeated
when they meet
their enemies
in the place of
judgement.

Psalm 127:5

Happy
are those,
O Lord,
whom you have
called
and chosen.

They will live
in your
sanctuary.

Psalm 65:4

Happy are those
who gain
wisdom
and prudence.

There is
more profit
in it than silver,
and it is worth
more than gold.

Proverbs 3:13

Happy are those
who obey
the Lord.

Those
who harden
their hearts
will give in
to evil.

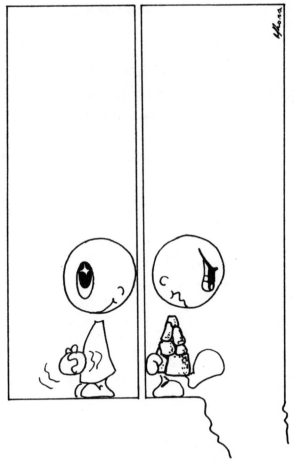

Proverbs 28:14

Happy are those who are kind to the poor.

It is a sin to despise your neighbour.

Proverbs 14:21

Happy is the husband
who has
a good wife;

he will live
twice as long
because of her.

Sirach 26:1

Happy are those
who become rich
through just means
and do not
worship
money.

They are
a wonder
and cause
for celebration
among the people.

Sirach 31:8

Happy are those who do not speak evil.

They are not
troubled
by the guilt
of sins.

Sirach 14:1

Happy are those
who have
a clear conscience

and who
never give up
hope.

Sirach 14:2

Happy are those
who cherish
wisdom
and use
good sense.

Those who study
the ways of
wisdom
will learn her
secrets.

Sirach 14:20

Happiness is the best gift
God has given to us,
for it is sharing
in God's own life.
GOD is
LIFE, BEAUTY
and FULLNESS.

GOD IS LOVE
and therefore
GOD IS JOY!

To be happy
we must let go
and abandon
ourselves to
God's love.

For the secret
of happiness is

Love

If I speak
in the tongues
of men and angels,

but
have no love,

... I am a booming gong
or a clanging cymbal

Love is

patient

Love is

kind

Love is

not jealous

not conceited

nor proud

not rude

nor selfish

not irritable

nor resentful

not happy
about injustice

but rejoices
in the truth

bears all things

believes all things

hopes all things

endures all things

1 Corinthians 13:4-7

Happy are those
who meditate
on these teachings.

Those who take them
to heart
will become wise.

Those who live by
these teachings
will be strong
at all times

for they will be
walking
in the light of
the Lord.

Sir. 50,28

DO YOU LOVE ME?

**A genial way of
presenting the Gospel...**

**The call of the Gospel
and Peter's response of love
illustrated with
an admirable sense of humour...**

The fascinating adventure of following Jesus and
the sweeping message of his teaching are, here,
narrated by Peter, the apostle who experienced
the unutterable joy of the answer to the call of
the Lord.

Peter's is the story of impassioned love –
unique. Reading its pages, everyone will be able
to grasp the criterion and the measure of true
and real love.

LATE HAVE
I LOVED YOU

ST AUGUSTINE

a man of God....
a man for others....

We all need someone to whom we can relate with our human experience, who shows us the way to find our true selves, who goes before us in the stupendous and arduous ways of God.
St Augustine has always been, for many, this Someone. His message, presented here in delightful images, is drawn mainly from the *Confessions of St Augustine,* one of the few books that still succeed in touching the heart of contemporary man and woman.

This is the **story of a call**, the 'inner' story of a
YES, in which, we are sure, all those 'who have
been called' will see themselves identified, and to
which others will certainly respond with shared
feelings.

With all my love

THE PSALMS

The Psalms are the hymns and prayers of the Bible. They include hymns of praise and worship of God; prayers for help, protection, and salvation; pleas for forgiveness; songs of thanksgiving.
But the theme that dominates all others in the Psalms is the love of God.
That love is illustrated in this book.